RicaTest

Subtest 1, 2 & 3 Study Guide

RICA Subtest 1, 2, & 3 Study Guide

Dear educator,

Welcome to the RICA Subtest 1, 2, & 3 Study Guide! We are thrilled to help you prepare for your RICA Test!

Written and edited by RicaTest.com.

RicaTest.com offers **volume discount keys for educational institutions** who are interested in using our test-preparation material for groups. For more information, please contact support@ricatest.com.

Become a Rica Test Ambassador

Find out how you can share our test preparation material and earn commissions at www.ricatest.com/ambassador.

Follow the RicaTest.com social accounts!

Facebook Group:

YouTube Channel:

Instagram:

rica_test

RicaTest

Rica Test Prep
Test Preparation Center
#ricatest
Official Rica Test prep!
Test-prep material to help you pass the Rica!
www.ricatest.com

Testimonials   Products   Subtest 1   Subtest 2   Case study   Subtest 3   FAQs

RicaTest .com

RICA Test Ambassador Program

Share RicaTest.com and get paid!

How It Works:

1. Login	2. Share	3. Get Paid!
Use your existing account	Tell teachers in your network	Receive recurring payment!

As a paid RICA Test customer, you are eligible to **become a RICA Test Ambassador.**

For every person that purchases our test preparation material using your individual link, **you receive recurring payment each month** they continue to use our product.

https://ricatest.com/ambassador/

About the RICA Test

The RICA Written Test is administered using three separate subtests.

RicaTest .com

Use the table and information below to better understand the RICA Written Test format.

RICA Test Structure

Subtest	Content Specifications Domains	Number of Competencies	Approximate Number of Multiple-Choice Items	Number and Type of Constructed-Response Items	Testing Time
1	**Domain 2** (Word Analysis)	5	27	1 (Focused Task, 150- to 300-word response)	
1	**Domain 3** (Fluency)	2	8	1 (Focused Task, 75- to 125-word response)	
	Subtest Total:	7	35	2	75 minutes
2	**Domain 4** (Vocabulary, Academic Language, and Background Knowledge)	2	19	1 (Focused Task, 75- to 125-word response)	
2	**Domain 5** (Comprehension)	4	16	1 (Focused Task, 150- to 300-word response)	
	Subtest Total:	6	35	2	75 minutes
3	**Domain 1** (Planning, Organizing, and Managing Reading Instruction Based on Ongoing Assessment)	2	25	1 (Case Study, 300- to 600-word response assessing all domains)	
	Subtest Total:	2	25	1	90 minutes

Purpose of the RICA Test

The RICA Test is an assessment given to people who want to become credentialed elementary teachers in California. The RICA Test checks teacher candidates' understanding of and ability to provide effective reading instruction to young learners in the classroom.

Length of Tests

- **Subtests I and II**: 1 hour and 15 minutes per subtest
- **Subtest III**: 1 hour and 30 minutes

Scoring Weight of Tests

- **Subtest 1:**
  - Multiple Choice: 85%
  - Essay 1: 5%
  - Essay 2: 10%
- **Subtest 2:**
  - Multiple Choice: 85%
  - Essay 1: 5%
  - Essay 2: 10%
- **Subtest 3:**
  - Multiple Choice: 80%
  - Case Study: 20%

RicaTest .com

How Subtests are Administered

Candidates who register to take more than one subtest in a single session at a physical test center are presented one subtest at a time.

Each subtest is individually timed and administered in consecutive order beginning with Subtest 1.

After you complete a subtest, you will not be able to return to a subtest.
- 15 additional minutes are provided to complete a nondisclosure agreement and tutorial.

Multiple-choice questions: All three subtests include a total of 95 multiple-choice questions. The multiple-choice questions are designed with four possible answers, but only one is the best choice.

It is important to read all of the available options and to select the best option, as there is no penalty for guessing.

Some multiple-choice questions include graphs, tables, charts, journal entries and other illustrations or diagrams, and you will want to quickly, but carefully review all the information to select the best possible answer.

Constructed-response questions: The typical format of the constructed-response, or essay questions includes the given information pertaining to and about a student's reading ability using a real-life situation, along with supplementary information in the form of charts and/or diagrams.

The test taker is then asked to discuss, describe, analyze, explain, or evaluate the given information and present a logical response, based on best practices for reading instruction.

Scoring: Reaching a score of 220 is considered a pass for each RICA subtest.
- *Multiple-choice questions* are scored electronically and tallied based on the number of questions answered correctly.

- *Constructed-response questions* are evaluated by a trained person who judges the overall effectiveness of the response, according to the characteristics of **reading instruction practices, teacher modeling, and student practice**.

Test-Taking Strategies

The RICA subtests allow the test takers to complete the test in the order (multiple-choice or essay questions) that best suits the examinee. For this reason, it is important to develop a test-taking strategy that works best for you.

On the one hand, you can work on the multiple-choice section and use a notepad to jot down reading instructional strategies and key terms as you move through the exam. Then, when it's time to write the constructed-responses, you will have an outline of content to refer to and use.

Take a moment and evaluate your own reading and writing speed and confidence for each skill. If you are a slower reader and a faster writer, it is wise to take the multiple choice section first, so that you make sure to complete the entire multiple choice section. If you feel confident in your understanding of the RICA specifications, key terms and reading strategies, it will be best to spend the first amount of time to thoroughly complete the constructed-response section.

Budget Your Time Well

The time you're given to complete each subtest goes by fast. It's important that you stay focused, read quickly, and answer questions as fast as you can while maintaining a high level of accuracy.

Here is the suggested timeframe that will help you budget your time well:

Subtest 1
- Multiple choice section: 35 minutes
- Short essay: 15 minutes
- Long essay: 25 minutes

Subtest 2
- Multiple choice section: 35 minutes
- Short essay: 15 minutes
- Long essay: 25 minutes

Subtest 3
- Multiple choice section: 30 minutes
- Case Study: 60 minutes

Completing the Multiple Choice Section

Prepare for difficult multiple-choice questions on the RICA Test. Read quickly, yet thoroughly; mark your best answer and move forward.

It's important that you remain calm and focused. Don't let frustration set in, and certainly don't make the mistake of spending too much time on a particular question.

Next, answer every question on the test. There is no penalty for answering a question incorrectly, so it is better to guess on a question than leave it blank.

Use the process of elimination. Remove answers that feel incorrect. Examine each word in the choices that remain, and select the best possible answer.

Writing Passing Essay Responses

There are a total of four essay questions, not including the Case Study. Within those four essay questions, two are shorter in length, and two are longer in length.

For the essay questions presented in Subtests 1 and 2, use this framework:
- **<u>Identify</u> one need demonstrated by the student described in the question.**
- **<u>Describe</u> an instructional strategy to address this student's need.**
- **<u>Explain</u> why the strategy you chose would effectively address this student's need.**

Remember the following:
- ☐ Using simple-to-understand words, while demonstrating your knowledge of reading instruction vocabulary.
- ☐ Answer every section of the essay question.
- ☐ Write concisely; don't be wordy.

Writing a Passing Case Study Response

The case study is covered extensively and completely in the online course. Watch, listen, and take notes to understand the examinee tasks and effective strategies to write a passing case study response.

Started by watching this video. Then, use the online course to master the material!

The 4 Most Important Questions To Know

1. What is it?
2. How do you teach it?
3. How do you assess it?
4. How do you differentiate a lesson to meet the needs of all learners?
   a. Struggling Readers
   b. English Learners
   c. Advanced Learners

More about the above questions:

The RICA Test covers a total of 13 fundamental reading instruction topics, which are listed below. It is absolutely crucial that you know the answers to the four questions listed above for each of the 13 topics below.

The end of every subtest study guide includes a list of student needs that are paired with the

- appropriate **definition** (*what it is*)
- **instructional strategy** (*how to teach it*)
- **assessment method** (*how to assess it*)
- **approach to differentiate the lesson** (how *to meet the needs of all learners*)

RicaTest.com

13 fundamental reading instruction topics

Organized by subtopic:

Subtest 1:

- Phonological awareness and phonemic awareness
- Concepts about print
- Letter recognition
- Alphabetic principle
- Phonics
- Sight words
- Syllabic and structural analysis
- Spelling (orthography)
- Fluency

Subtest 2:

- Vocabulary, including academic/non-academic language, and background knowledge
- Comprehension- literary texts
- Comprehension- expository texts

Subtest 3:

- General reading strategies and assessments

5 Reading Tips To Boost Your Score

Read faster and comprehend more with these reading tips:

RicaTest .com

1. Have a clear mind

We all have a lot of things on our mind. Before entering the testing space, do a conscious check of how you are feeling and remind yourself that you will have time to think of other things later, but now it's time to focus on the test.

2. Read quickly, and thoroughly

You cannot comprehend that which you did not read.

The RICA Test writers place an emphasis on every word. This means that each word counts, so you've got to read everything. Each question includes a lot of information and oftentimes the most important aspect of the question can be the easiest to overlook.

You need to know each question in its entirety, but you also need to get through the test quickly. For this, read fast, and be focused.

3. Take notes

While taking the RICA Test, you are allowed to jot down notes as they come up, both in your head as well as from the exam.

Use the scratch pad that is given in order to take notes to record important bits of information as you find them in your test for both the multiple-choice section as well as the constructed-response section.

4. Look at structure

When reading possible multiple-choice answers, examine not only the words, but also the structure of each choice.

Oftentimes but not all the time, the first word of each solution helps you select the best two of the four possibilities. Narrowing down your answer to two options will allow you a better chance to select the one correct answer.

5. Stay calm and move at a consistent pace

Consistency is key, and a stable pace with a clear focus will allow you to perform at your highest level. You've got this!

RICA Test Frequently Asked Questions

Below you will find the most commonly asked RICA Test questions and their answers.

What is the RICA test?

The RICA test stands for Reading Instruction Competence Assessment. It is a test taken by California elementary teachers and education specialists in order to obtain a teaching credential.

Who needs to take the RICA test?

People who complete the Multiple Subject Teaching Credential or Educational Specialist Instruction Credential programs in California need to take and pass the RICA test.

How long do RICA results take?

If you take the RICA test in-person, at a designated Pearson testing center, results come back within four weeks.

If you take the test remotely, the test results come back within three weeks.

What happens if you can't pass the RICA?

Passing the RICA is tough! However, you are able to take the test as many times as you need. However, you are required to wait 45 days from your original test date before you can retest.

What is a passing score on the RICA?

Although the RICA test is now split into three subtests, the passing score is still 220.

How much does the RICA test cost?

Each subtest costs $57, or a total of $171 for all three tests.

What are the 5 domains of the RICA?

- **Domain 1**: Planning, Organizing, and Managing Reading Instruction Based on Ongoing Assessment
- **Domain 2**: Word Analysis
- **Domain 3**: Fluency
- **Domain 4**: Vocabulary, Academic Language, Background Knowledge
- **Domain 5**: Comprehension

When should I take the RICA exam?

People are allowed to take the RICA exam at any time; however, for purposes of planning to find a full-time teaching position, teachers will want to make sure they have received a passing score before they graduate from their Multiple-Subjects Teaching Credential Program.

What do I need to know for the RICA?

The RICA is a large test that is made up of a lot of information. The exam is built to assess a teacher's understanding of providing effective reading instruction, so knowing about teaching reading to elementary-aged students will be necessary.

What is the RICA video performance assessment?

The most popular RICA test for teachers is the written test; however, the California Commission on Teacher Credentialing also accepts a video submission in place of taking the written exam.

The CTC states, "The RICA Video Performance Assessment offers candidates the option of an evaluation based on actual classroom performance rather than a written examination. Candidates who choose the Video Performance Assessment create and submit video recordings of themselves teaching reading."

Can you take the RICA online?

Yes! You can now take the RICA test online.

RICA Subtest 1 Study Guide

To be fully prepared to pass the RICA Subtest 1, which includes RICA domain 2 (Word Analysis) and domain 3 (Fluency), you will want to read the questions and answers below carefully to understand the material that will be covered in subtest number 1.

Subtest 1 - Structure

The table below shows that Subtest 1 consists of reading Domain 2 and 3, which includes Word Analysis and Fluency.

Domain	Number of competencies	Number of Multiple-Choice Questions	Number and Type of Constructed-Response Questions
Domain 2 (Word Analysis)	5	27	1 CRQ; 150- to 300-word response
Domain 3 (Fluency)	2	8	1 CRQ; 75- to 125-word response
Total	7	35	2

Between the two domains, there are a total of seven reading competencies to know that will be covered with 35 multiple-choice questions.

Along with the multiple-choice questions, Subtest 1 also includes a total of two essays, or constructed-response questions (CRQs). The first CRQ will ask you a question related to a topic that derives from Domain 2, where you're instructed to compose a 150- to 300-word response. The second CRQ comes from a topic related to Domain 2's content, which asks for a 75- to 125, respectively.

Subtest 1 - Overview

Below, you will find the competencies that make up each of the domains that you must know to pass subtest 1:

Domain 2: Word Analysis

Competency 3: Understand the role of phonological and phonemic awareness in reading development and how to develop students' phonological and phonemic awareness skills.

Competency 4: Understand the role of concepts about print, letter recognition, and the alphabetic principle in reading development and how to develop students' knowledge and skills in these areas.

Competency 5: Understand important terminology and concepts involved in phonics instruction and recognize the role of phonics and sight words in reading development.

Competency 6: Understand how to develop students' phonics knowledge and skills and recognition of sight words to promote accurate word analysis that leads to automaticity in word recognition and contributes to spelling development.

Competency 7: Understand the role of syllabic and structural analysis and orthographic knowledge in reading development and how to develop students' knowledge and skills in these areas to promote accurate word analysis that leads to automaticity in word recognition and contributes to spelling development.

Domain 3: Fluency

Competency 8: Understand the role of fluency in reading development and factors that affect students' development of fluency.

Competency 9: Understand how to promote students' fluency development.

Subtest 1 - Learning Outcomes

Be able to answer the following questions:

1. What is the difference between phonological awareness to phonemic awareness and phonics?

2. How to teach phonemic awareness?

3. How to assess phonemic awareness?

4. How to differentiate phonemic awareness instruction for *struggling readers, English Learners,* and *advanced learners*

5. What are the four Concepts About Print?

6. How to teach Concepts About Print?

7. How to assess Concepts About Print?

8. How to differentiate Concepts About Print instruction for *struggling readers, English learners,* and *advanced learners.*

9. Describe the difference between *letter recognition, letter naming, letter formation,* and *alphabetic principle.*

10. Describe *letter recognition,* including what it is, the importance of it in reading development, how to teach it, how to assess it, and how to differentiate instruction for it.

11. Describe *phonics,* including what it is, the importance of it in reading development, which words are taught as sight words, how to teach it, how to assess it, and how to differentiate instruction for it.

12. What is the difference between structural analysis and syllabic analysis?

13. How to teach, assess, and differentiate structural analysis?

14. What is orthography, how to teach it, assess it, and differentiate instruction for it?

15. What are the three key aspects of reading fluency?

16. Define *automaticity theory.*

17. Describe how to teach, assess and differentiate fluency instruction.

18. How to teach and assess for accuracy in reading fluency?

19. How to teach and assess rate in reading fluency?

20. How to teach and assess prosody in reading fluency?

21. What is the main cause for poor reading fluency?

RICA Subtest 1
Study Guide Answers

1. What is the difference between phonological awareness, phonemic awareness and phonics?
   - **Phonological awareness**: The understanding that oral English is made up of small units
   - **Phonemic awareness**: The ability to distinguish individual sounds in a word
   - **Phonics**: The knowledge of letter-to-sound correspondence

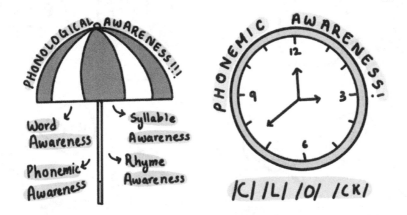

=> PHONICS <=

RicaTest .com

2. How to teach phonemic awareness?

    a. Sound isolation: Teacher gives student a word, and asks student to isolate the beginning, middle, or ending sound.

        i. "What is the beginning sound of *bat?*" /b/

    b. Sound blending: Teacher says the sounds of a word with brief pauses between each sound and asks student, "Which word is it?"

        i. /b/, /a/, /t/ = bat

    c. Sound segmentation: Teacher says a word and asks student to segment, or break up, the word through its sounds

        i. Teacher says, "*bat.*" Student says, "/b/, /a/, /t/"

3. How to assess phonemic awareness?

Start with sound segmentation. Formal test is called Yopp-Singer Test. If that is too difficult for the student, move backward to sound blending; if that is too difficult, move back to sound isolation

RicaTest .com

Y opp

S inger

T est

#1
Sound Isolation
↓
#2
Sound Blending
↓
#3
Sound Segmentation
OR YST

⇒ Assess Phonemic Awareness

4. How to differentiate phonemic awareness instruction for *struggling readers, English Learners,* and *advanced learners*

- **Struggling readers:** Focus on key skills using sound blending and sound segmenting
- **English Learners:** Teach phonemes that do not exist in English Learner's first language
- **Advanced readers:** Increase pace of instruction and build on current skills

STRUGGLING → LEARNERS → ADVANCED

/k/ /ă/ /t/

/sh/ /i/ /p/

/l/ /i/ /t/

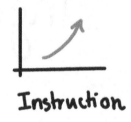

Instruction

5. What are the four Concepts About Print?

a. Print carries **meaning**
b. Letter, word, and sentence **representation**
c. **Directionality**- ability to track print
d. **Book-handling skills**

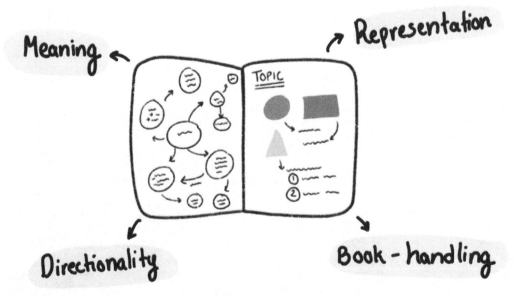

6. How to teach Concepts About Print

Shared book experience:

- Teacher uses a Big Book and starts by introducing the cover, author's name, title, title page, and other aspects of the book
- Teacher reads story with full dramatic punch. Teacher pauses for predictions
- Teacher and students have a discussion about the book, sharing their favorite parts
- Story is reread at a later time, where students can reenact parts of the story

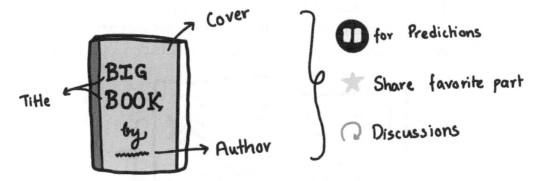

7. How to assess Concepts About Print

   a. Teacher picks a picture book and has pencil and paper for teacher

   b. Teacher asks students questions like, "*Can you show me where I should start to read?*

   c. Also, teacher asks students to point to the words as the teacher reads them **to assess directionality**

   d. **To assess word boundaries**, teacher covers up all lines except one, and asks student, "H*ow many words are on this line?*"

   e. **To assess if a child understands that print carries meaning**, teacher asks student to write something. If child writes letters (not squiggles or pictures), the child demonstrates the understanding that letters convey meaning

8. How to differentiate Concepts About Print instruction for *struggling readers, English learners,* and *advanced learners*

- **For struggling readers**: Use tactile and kinesthetic methods, such as using letter tiles to help tell the difference between a letter and a word
- **For English Learners**: Use knowledge from student's L1 to transfer skills to English instruction
- **For advanced learners**: Increase the pace of instruction and/or build on and extend current knowledge and skills

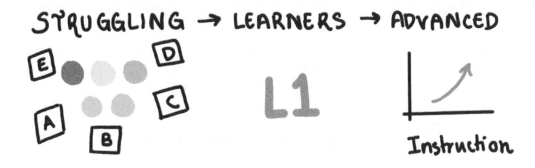

9. Describe the difference between *letter recognition, letter naming, letter formation,* and *alphabetic principle*

- **Letter recognition:** The ability for a student to identify upper and lowercase letters when a teacher says the name of the letter (teacher says, student points)
- **Letter naming:** The ability for a student to say the name of a letter when the teacher points (teacher points, student says)
- **Letter formation:** Also called *letter production;* the ability for a student to write the uppercase and lowercase letters legibly
- **Alphabetic principle:** The understanding that in English, letters represent sounds

LETTER

Recognition → A vs. a

Naming → "A" → "Ae"

Formation → ✎ A vs. a

_____

Alphabetic Principle → A = •◂))

10. Describe *letter recognition,* including what it is, the importance of it in reading development, how to teach it, how to assess it, and how to differentiate instruction for it

- **What is it**: The ability to identify the upper and lowercase letters when a teacher says the name of the letter. (Teacher says, *"Point to the big A";* student points)
- **The importance of letter recognition for reading development**: Letters are the building blocks of printed language, and students must be able to identify letters in order to succeed in later reading instruction, such as in phonics
- **How to teach letter recognition:** Use methods that are tactile and kinesthetic, such as when kids use modeling clay to make letters. This method also works great for struggling readers.
- **How to assess letter recognition:**
  - Teacher has a list of all 26 letters.
  - Teacher orally asks student to, *"Point to the big f."* and student points.
- **How to differentiate instruction for letter recognition:**
  - **For struggling readers**: Use tactile and kinesthetic methods, such as having the child write letters with his bare finger on the desktop or in sand
  - **For English Learners**: Use knowledge from student's L1 to transfer skills to English instruction
  - **For advanced learners**: Increase the pace of instruction and/or build on and extend current knowledge and skills

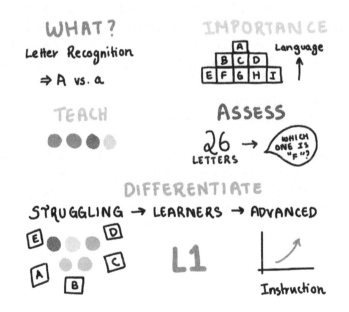

11. Describe *phonics,* including what it is, the importance of it in reading development, which words are taught as sight words, how to teach it, how to assess it, and how to differentiate instruction for it

- **What is it?** The instruction to teach children the correct sound-to-symbol relationships in the English language
- **The importance of phonics for reading development**: knowledge of phonics aids students with more smooth and accurate word identification, which increases reading fluency that helps reading comprehension
- **Which words are taught as sight words:** high-frequency words, irregularly spelt words, words that children want to know, words introduced in content areas, like history and science
- **How to teach it?** Use Whole-to-Part Instruction
  - Teacher writes sentences on board, each having common element underlined
  - Teacher and students read each sentence aloud
  - Students read aloud underlined word (target language= TL)
  - Teacher circles target language, and students make the sound of TL
  - Teacher and student repeat with next sentences
- **How to assess it?**
  - **In isolation**: Teacher presents student with list of words with common element (words with *sh)* and student reads the words
  - **In context:** Teacher presents student with a 2-3 paragraph passage and asks students to read. Teacher listens for miscues and notes patterns
- **How to differentiate phonics instruction for struggling readers, English learners, and advanced learners?**
  - **For struggling readers:** Focus on key phonics and high-frequency words, and slow down the pace of instruction, reteach skills that are lacking, use concrete examples, provide additional practice
  - **For English learners:** Use transferable knowledge from L1, and explicitly teach sounds and meanings that do not transfer
  - **Advanced learners:** Increase the pace and/or complexity of instruction, and build on existing knowledge and skills

WHAT?

PHONICS | 👁 words
•)) → Aa | ↑ freq. words

IMPORTANCE

⟹ Smooth + Easy
"word identification"
= ↑ fluency

TEACH

◯ → ▷
Whole - to - Part

ASSESS

① Isolation
② In context

DIFFERENTIATE

STRUGGLING → LEARNERS → ADVANCED

↑〰〰 words

↓ Instruction
pace

L1

Instruction

12. What is the difference between structural analysis and syllabic analysis?

- ○ **Structural Analysis:** Students decode a word using their knowledge of the root word in combination with the word's affix (prefix or suffix)
- ○ **Syllabic Analysis:** Students decode a word using their knowledge of the syllables of the word

STRUCTURAL   vs.   SYLLABIC

STRUCTURAL	SYLLABIC
Prefix → hyper- extra- under-	nap | kin
	ro | bot
Suffix → - ing - ly - ness	can | dle
	com | plex
	ca | bin

13. How to teach, assess, and differentiate structural analysis?

- **How to teach it?** Use Whole-to-Part Method to teach root words and affixes
  - Teacher writes sentences on the board with target words underlined
  - Teacher and students read sentences, and teacher circles target root or affix
  - Teacher and students try to arrive at meaning
  - Teacher provides other words with common root word or affix, and ask if students can think of more words with common element
- **How to assess it?**
  - **In isolation**: Teacher gives traditional spelling test
  - **In context:** Teacher uses student's writing passage and notes patterns of errors
- **How to differentiate instruction for structural analysis?**
  - **Struggling readers:** Teach key skills and how to spell and pronounce common prefixes, suffixes, and root words
  - **English Learners:** (same as above) Teach key skills and how to spell and pronounce common prefixes, suffixes, and root words
  - **Advanced learners:** Increase pace of instruction and build on existing skills

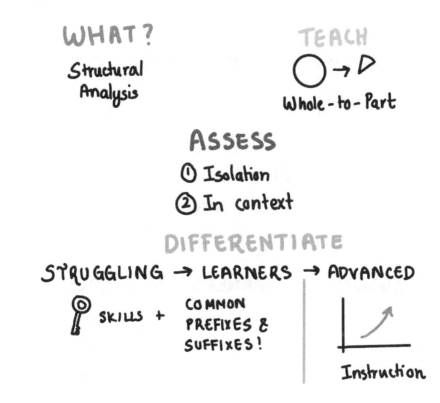

14. What is orthography, how to teach it, assess it, and differentiate instruction for it?

- **What is it?** Orthography is the ability to spell words correctly
- **How to teach it?** Use Multisensory Instruction
  - Students write the target word(s) multiple times using different colors and highlight the target element (boat) [visual] while saying each letter aloud [auditory]
- **How to assess it?**
  - **In isolation**: Teacher gives traditional spelling test
  - **In context:** Teacher uses student's writing passage and notes patterns of errors
- **Differentiation for:**
  - **Struggling readers**: focus on most important spelling skills and patterns that the student will see often, such as, *pre-, sub-*
    - Use tactile approaches to teach
  - **English learners**: explicitly teach learners English roots and affixes
  - **Advanced learners:** Increase the pace of instruction, and build onto existing skills

WHAT?

Orthography

= √ spelling

TEACH

MULTISENSORY INSTRUCTION

👁 vs. 👂

ASSESS

① Isolation

② In context

DIFFERENTIATE

STRUGGLING → LEARNERS → ADVANCED

☆ Skills + Patterns

English Roots + Affixes

Instruction

15. What are the three key aspects of reading fluency?

Accuracy, rate, and prosody

RicaTest .com

16. Define *automaticity theory*

Automaticity theory is the ability of a student to **decode words** and **understand the meaning of the text** which was read

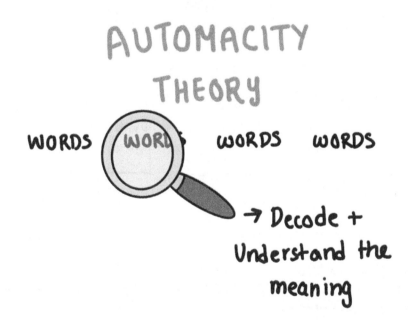

17. Describe how to teach, assess and differentiate fluency instruction

- **What is it?** The ability to read with accuracy, proper rate and prosody
- **How to teach it?** Monitored Oral Reading
  - Teacher models proper oral reading and students listen
  - Students practice reading the same text aloud
  - Teacher gives feedback
- **How to assess it?** Assessed through oral reading only
  - Use an Oral Reading Fluency test, count the words read per minute

RicaTest .com

- **How to differentiate fluency instruction?**
  - **For struggling readers:**
    - Use texts at students' independent reading level
    - Improve accuracy through word identification instruction
    - Focus on sight word recognition
    - Improve rate through additional reading practice
  - **For English learners:**
    - Teach tonal patterns and rhythms of English using Echo Reading, where teacher reads aloud, then student reads it aloud with the teacher, focusing in on pronunciation
  - **For advanced learners**
    - Increase the pace of instruction
    - Use more advanced texts

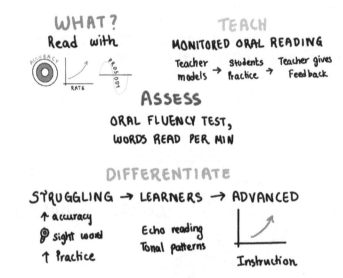

18. How to teach and assess for accuracy in reading fluency?

- **How to teach accuracy:** Build automatic word identification skills
  - Use phonemic awareness, phonics and sight word instruction
- **How to assess accuracy?** Use Running Records and identify patterns in student's miscues
  - Use an **Oral Reading Fluency test** to count the words read per minute

WHAT?
Reading fluency

ACCURACY

TEACH
1. Build word identification skills
2. Running records + patterns in student's miscues

ASSESS
ORAL FLUENCY TEST

19. How to teach and assess rate in reading fluency?

- **How to teach rate**: Use whisper reading
  - Student's read aloud in whisper voice
  - Teacher walks around, listens, and gives feedback
- **How to assess rate**: Use timed reading
  - Teacher uses one-minute reading sample
  - Teacher listens to student's oral reading and notes miscues
  - Total number of words read minus total number of reading errors = WCPA

WHAT?

Reading fluency

RATE

TEACH

WHISPER READING

ASSESS

TIMED
READING

20. How to teach and assess prosody in reading fluency?

- **How to teach prosody**: Use Phrase-Cued Reading
  - Teacher makes marks in text passage
    - / = comma; // = period
  - Students with same independent reading level come together in small group
  - Students practice reading using teacher's markings for proper prosody
- **How to assess prosody**:
  - Teacher listens to student read aloud while listening for miscue patterns in prosody

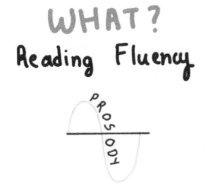

WHAT?
Reading Fluency
PROSODY

TEACH
Phrase - Cued
Reading
) → short pause
• → long pause

ASSESS
Teacher ()) to student for
〜〜 patterns in prosody

21. What is the main cause for poor reading fluency?

Weak word analysis skills

RICA Subtest 1 -
Essay Question Study Guide

Subtest 1 includes a total of two essays, or constructed-response questions, that you're asked to compose a 150- to 300-word response for Domain 2's questions and a 75- to 125-word response for Domain 3's question, respectively.

RicaTest .com

Understanding a student's strengths and/or needs and being able to present instructional strategies and the benefits of the instructional strategies to support the student's reading development will be a major advantage in your writing successful essays.

Below is a list of student needs you may find in your RICA Test.

*Note- There are multiple instructional strategies that can be used; however, you should choose to write about the one instructional strategy that you feel most comfortable to explain.

Student's needs and instructional strategies for phonemic awareness:

- **Student's need:** The student is having a difficult time identifying how many words are in a sentence
  - ○ **Instructional strategy**: Build word awareness skills
    - Teacher uses several cards, each having one word written on it
    - Teacher creates two-word sentences, *Jack walks*
    - Teacher and student read sentence together
    - Teacher splits sentence up by words
    - Teacher asks student, "How many words are in the sentence?"
    - Teacher builds off sentence and adds a word to create three-word sentence, *Jack walks fast*
    - Teacher asks, "How many words are in the sentence?"
  - ○ **Benefit:** Helps children become aware that sentences are made up of words

- **Student's need:** The student is having a difficult time identifying syllables in a word
  - ○ **Instructional strategy**: Build syllable awareness skills
    - Teach children to clap their hands as they say each syllable in a word
    - Pronounce words slowly and elongate word pronunciation
  - ○ **Benefit:** Helps children become aware that words are made up of syllables

- **Student's need**: The student is having difficulty with compound words
  - ○ **Instructional strategy**: Build word blending skills

- Teacher has pictures of the two parts of the compound word (foot, ball)
- Teacher prompts, "This is a picture of a foot, and this is a picture of a ball, what do you get when you put them together?" (football)
  - **Benefit:** Helps children visually see compound words

- **Student's need:** The student is having difficulty reading multisyllabic words
  - **Instructional strategy:** Build syllable blending skills
    - Teacher says, "What word do we give if we put *bro* and *ther* together?" (brother)
  - **Benefit:** Helps students put multisyllabic words together

- **Student's need:** The student is having difficulty identifying the sounds at the beginning, middle, or end of a word
  - **Instructional strategy:** Build sound isolation skills
    - Teacher picks a list of words with a common element that student has shown a need to improve, such as words with the long a sound
    - Teacher models correct pronunciation of the word and says the sound of the problem element, in this case, the long a sound
    - Teacher says a word (more challenging if the student needs to read the word), and the student pronounces the word, and gives the beginning, middle, or ending sound (whichever the lesson is focused on)
  - **Benefit:** Helps students break up sounds of a word

- **Student's need:** The student is having a difficult time reading multisyllabic words
  - **Instructional strategy:** Build sound blending skills
    - Teacher says sounds of words with brief pauses between each sound, /c/, /a/, /t/
    - Teacher says, "Which word am I thinking of?" (cat)
  - **Benefit:** Helps students properly pronounce new words

- **Student's need:** The student is having a difficult time isolating and identifying the sounds in a spoken word
  - **Instructional strategy**: Build sound segmentation skills
    - Teacher starts by gathering a list of words with only two sounds
    - Teacher models desired behavior by saying, "I am going to say a word and then say the sounds in the word."
      - *Bee, /b/, /e/*
    - Once student demonstrates ability with two-sound words, teacher uses words with three sounds
      - *Cat, /c/, /a/, /t/*
  - **Benefit:** Helps students segment new words

Student's needs in and instructional strategies for concepts about print:

- **Student's need:** The student is having a difficult time with awareness between the relationship that print carries meaning, letter, word, and sound representation, directionality of print, AND/OR book-handling skills
  - **Instructional strategy**: Use shared book experience
    - Teacher uses a Big Book and starts by introducing the cover, author's name, title, title page, and other aspects of the book
    - Teacher reads story with full dramatic punch. Teacher pauses for predictions
    - Teacher and students have a discussion about the book, sharing their favorite parts
    - Story is reread at a later time, where students can reenact parts of the story
  - **Benefit:** Helps students improve all aspects of concepts about print

- **Student's need**: The student is having a difficult time recognizing, naming and/or writing specific letters
  - **Instructional strategy:** Use tactile and kinesthetic methods, such as when kids use modeling clay to make letters. This method also works great for struggling readers
  - **Benefit:** Hands-on approach to better understanding and becoming familiar with letters

- **Student's need**: The student is mixing up similar letters, such as p, d, q, and/or b
  - ○ **Instructional strategy:** Use tactile, kinesthetic, auditory and visual methods
    - ■ Teacher models and provides students practice to trace and write the target letters while students say out loud the direction it takes to make the letter. This can be done on screens to make the activity tactile, can be done in the air to make the activity kinesthetic, and can be done using different colored crayons or colored pencils to make the activity visual
  - ○ **Benefit:** Hands-on approach to better understanding and becoming familiar with letters

- **Student's need:** The student is having a difficult time with phonics and/or sight words
  - ○ **Instructional strategy**: Use whole-to-part phonics/ sight word instruction (see above for specific directions)
  - ○ **Benefit:** Gives students systematic, direct and explicit instruction toward understanding the relationship between sound-to-writing of language

- **Student's need:** The student is struggling with root words or affixes (prefixes/ suffixes)
  - ○ **Instructional strategy**: Use whole-to-part structural analysis instruction (see above for specific directions)
  - ○ **Benefit:** Gives students systematic, direct and explicit instruction toward understanding the parts of a written word

- **Student's need**: The student is struggling with spelling
  - ○ **Instructional strategy:** Use Multisensory Instruction
    - ■ Students having a difficult time spelling should write the target word(s) multiple times using different colors by highlighting the target vowels (boat) [visual] while saying each word out loud [auditory]
  - ○ **Benefit:** Caters to student's senses to help remember spelling better

RicaTest .com

- **Student's need**: The student isn't motivated about reading
  - ○ **Instructional strategy**: Use I + I strategy (student's **interest** + student's **independent reading level**)
  - ○ **Benefit:** Caters to student's interest

Student's needs in and instructional strategies for fluency:

- **Student's need:** The student needs to improve reading fluency
  - ○ **Instructional strategy**: Use Monitored Oral Reading
  - ○ **Benefit:** Provides student with modeling, practice and feedback

- **Student's need:** The student needs to improve reading fluency, specifically with accuracy
  - ○ **Instructional strategy:** Use Monitored Oral Reading
    - ■ **Build word identification skills**, such as phonics and sight words
  - ○ **Benefit:** Provides student with modeling, practice and feedback

- **Student's need:** The student needs to improve reading fluency, specifically with rate
  - ○ **Instructional strategy:** Use Monitored Oral Reading
    - ■ Whisper reading
  - ○ **Benefit:** Encourages reading, even for shy/embarrassed readers

- **Student's need:** The student needs to improve reading fluency, specifically with prosody
  - ○ **Instructional strategy:** Use Monitored Oral Reading
    - ■ Phrase-cued reading
      - Teacher makes marks in text passage
        - ○ / = comma; // = period
      - Students with the same independent reading level come together in small group

RicaTest .com

- Students practice reading using teacher's markings for proper prosody
  - **Benefit:** Provides student with modeling, practice and feedback

RICA Subtest 2 Study Guide

To be fully prepared to pass the RICA Subtest 2, which includes RICA Domain 4 (Vocabulary, Academic Language, and Background Knowledge) and Domain 5 (Comprehension), read this guide carefully to understand the material that will be covered in Subtest 2.

Subtest 2 - Structure

The table below shows that Subtest 2 consists of reading Domain 4 and 5, which includes Word Analysis and Fluency.

Domain	Number of competencies	Number of Multiple-Choice Questions	Number and Type of Constructed-Response Questions
Domain 4 (Vocabulary, Academic Language, and Background Knowledge)	2	19	1 CRQ; 75- to 125-word response
Domain 5 (Comprehension)	4	16	1 CRQ; 150- to 300-word response
Total	**6**	**35**	**2**

Between the two domains, there are a total of six reading competencies to know that will be covered with 35 multiple-choice questions.

Subtest 2 also includes a total of two essays, or constructed-response questions, that you're asked to compose a 75- to 125-word response for Domain 4's question and a 150- to 300-word response for Domain 5's question, respectively.

Subtest 2 - Overview

Below, you will find the competencies that make up each of the domains that you must know to pass Subtest 2:

Domain 4: Vocabulary, Academic Language, and Background Knowledge

Competency 10: Vocabulary, Academic Language, and Background Knowledge: Role in Reading Development and Factors that Affect their Development.

Competency 11: Vocabulary, Academic Language, and Background Knowledge: Instruction and Assessment.

Domain 5:

Competency 12: Understand literal, inferential, and evaluative comprehension and factors affecting reading comprehension.

Competency 13: Understand how to facilitate reading comprehension by providing instruction that prepares students for the reading task, scaffolds them as needed through the reading process, and prepares them to respond to what they have read.

Competency 14: Understand how to promote students' comprehension and analysis of narrative/literary texts and their development of literary response skills.

Competency 15: Understand how to promote students' comprehension of expository/informational texts and their development of study skills and research skills.

Subtest 2 - Learning Outcomes

Be able to answer the following questions:

1. What is the difference between technical and non-technical academic language?

2. How to teach, assess, and differentiate vocabulary instruction?

3. What are the factors to consider when teaching new vocabulary?

4. What are the three types of reading comprehension, and their meanings?

5. How to teach reading comprehension before reading?

6. What is an instructional strategy for and the method to access comprehension of a narrative text?

7. What is an instructional strategy for and the method to access comprehension of an expository text?

8. What to do when a student is struggling with predicting, generating questions, clarifying, or summarizing?

9. How to assess and differentiate instruction for reading comprehension?

10. If you need an oral activity to access reading comprehension, which strategy can you use?

11. If you need a written activity to access reading comprehension, which strategy can you use?

12. How to differentiate reading comprehension of literary instruction?

13. What is the difference between skimming and scanning?

14. How to teach, assess, and differentiate reading comprehension for expository texts?

15. What is the Matthew Effect?

16. What are the four components of vocabulary instruction?

17. What is word consciousness?

18. What are the 5 stages of spelling development and how are they related?

RICA Subtest 2
Study Guide Answers

1. What is the difference between technical and non-technical academic language?

- **Technical academic language:** Words related to specific subjects, like sovereignty, monarchy, tyranny
- **Non-technical academic language:** Words that run across multiple disciplines, such as theory, hypothesis, analysis

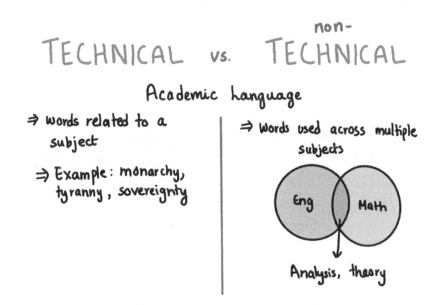

2. What is vocabulary instruction, how to teach it, assess it, and differentiate instruction for it?

- **What is it?** Vocabulary is the set of words and phrases that a student is able to use and understand
- **How to teach it?** Use Contextual Redefinition
  - Teacher displays text passage that highlights to-be-taught vocabulary
  - Students independently read the passage and write what they think the meaning of the vocabulary words are. If students don't know, they write, I don't know.
  - Students move into small groups of three, share their definitions of the words, and each student is free to change or update their definition
  - Teacher moves instruction back to whole-group, and asks for volunteer students to read their definitions

RicaTest.com

- Teacher listens to students and writes definition of the word on the board and the students copy it into their word journals
- **How to assess it?** Use standardized vocabulary test
  - Test should use vocab words in context and have multiple choice options
- **How to differentiate vocabulary instruction:**
  - **For struggling readers:**
    - Focus on key vocabulary and nontechnical academic language
    - Reteach what is not mastered
    - Provide concrete examples
    - Use visual, kinesthetic, and tactile activities
  - **For English Learners:**
    - Use transfer of L1 (cognates)
    - Provide concrete examples
  - **For advanced learners:**
    - Increase the pace of instruction
    - Use more advanced texts
    - Extend the assignments

3. What are the factors to consider when teaching new vocabulary?

1) **Frequency** the students will see the word

2) **Utility** of how important the word will be to the students

RicaTest.com

3) **Level of knowledge,** the less students know about a word and the more useful it is to them, the more important it is to teach

4. What are the three types of reading comprehension, and their meanings?

- **Literal comprehension:** Understanding the surface meaning of the text. Literal comprehension questions are ones that the answers are in the text
- **Inferential comprehension:** Understanding something that was implied through the text. Inferential comprehension questions require the reader to speculate, or infer, meaning
- **Evaluative comprehension:** Understanding the implications of a character, or the lesson of the story by requiring the reader to make a judgment from the text

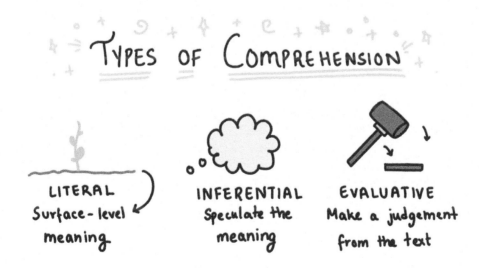

5. How to teach reading comprehension before reading?

Activate students' background knowledge:

- **KWL chart**: Teacher writes KWL on chart paper and separates the three letters with a line, forming three columns. K represents what students know, W for what students want to know, and L for what students want to learn.
- **Picture walk**: Teacher has a book and the teacher and students "walk through the book" by looking at the pictures of the story ahead of time to get a gist of what the story is about.
- **Set purpose for reading**: Teacher directly and explicitly states, *"Today class, we are going to read about friendship..."*

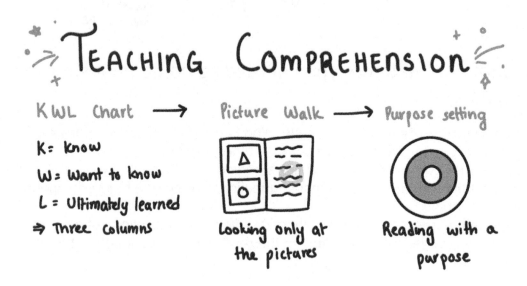

6. What is an instructional strategy for and the method to access comprehension of a narrative text?

Instructional strategy:

- **For younger learners:** Use retelling (best for younger because oral)
- **For older learners:** Use story grammar outline (best for older because written)
    - **SGO helps students identify literary elements**
        - *Setting:*
        - *Characters:*
        - *Problem:*
            - *event 1:*
            - *event 2:*
            - *event 3:*
        - *Resolution:*
        - *Theme:*

Assessment strategy: Use Question-Answer Relationships (QAR)

- **For K-1st grade:**
    - In the book (literal comprehension)
    - In my head (inferential and/or evaluative comprehension)
- **For 2nd-6th grade:**
    - **To access literal comprehension:** *Right there* (answer is in the text located in one section)
    - **To access literal comprehension:** *Think and search* (answer is in the text located in two sections)
    - **To access inferential and/or evaluative comprehension**: *Author and Me* (must use knowledge from the text to answer the question)
    - **To access inferential and/or evaluative comprehension:** *On My Own* (answer is not in story- reader needs to detect bias or distinguish fact from opinion)
- **For middle schoolers-** teacher and students use the following terms:
    - Literal question
    - Inferential question
    - Evaluative question

INSTRUCTIONAL STRATEGY

narrative text

YOUNG

↻ Retelling

⇒ Oral form

OLDER

☰ Story-grammar outline

⇒ Written

ASSESS

? Question-Answer Relationships (QAR).

STRATEGY

K-1 → Book + Head

2-6 grade → Right there, Think & Search, Author & me, On my Own

Middle School → Literal, Evaluative & Inferential Qs.

---

7. What is an instructional strategy for and the method to access comprehension of an expository text?

Instructional strategy:

- Teach expository text structures- *cause and effect, problem and solution, compare and contrast, etc…*
- Teach text features- *table of contents, index, glossary, etc...*
- **Before reading:** Use **KWL chart**
- **During reading:** Use graphic organizer

Assessment strategy: Use Question-Answer Relationships Study Guide (QAR)

Use Question Classification/ Answer Verification Study Guide (three-level study guide with literal, inferential, and evaluative questions)

- **For K-1st grade:**
    - In the book (literal comprehension)
    - In my head (inferential and/or evaluative comprehension)
- **For 2nd-6th grade:**
    - **To access literal comprehension:** *Right there* (answer in the text in one section)
    - **To access literal comprehension:** *Think and search* (answer in the text in two sections)
    - **To access inferential and/or evaluative comprehension**: *Author and Me* (use knowledge from the text to answer)

RicaTest.com

- To access inferential and/or evaluative comprehension: *On My Own* (answer is not in story- reader needs to detect bias or distinguish fact from opinion)
- **For middle schoolers** (teacher and students use the following terms)
  - Literal question
  - Inferential question
  - Evaluative question

expository text

INSTRUCTION

⇒ Expository text Structures

⇒ Text features

Before : KWL Chart

During : Graphic Organizer

ASSESS

? Question-Answer Relationships (QAR).

STRATEGY

K-1 → Book + Head

2-6 grade → Right there, Think & Search, Author & me, On my Own

Middle School → Literal, Evaluative & Inferential Qs.

8. What to do when a student is struggling with predicting, generating questions, clarifying, or summarizing?

Use gradual release of responsibility

- Teacher starts by doing most of the work
- Gradually releases responsibility to the students
- Teacher models target strategy
- Teacher uses think-alouds: *"I'm going to make a prediction."*
- Teacher uses scaffolds (support) to offer students' options

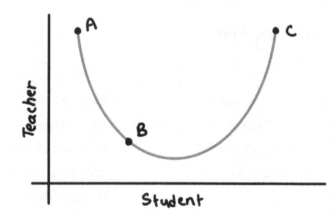

A = Teacher does most of the work

B = Gradual release of responsibility to student

C = Student stops struggling

9. How to assess and differentiate instruction for reading comprehension?

To access using oral: Question-Answer Relationships

- *For K-1st grade:*
  - **In the book** (or)
  - **In my head**
- *For 2nd-6th grade:*
  - **Right there**
  - **Think and search**
  - **Author and You**
  - **On My Own**

To access using written: Write a summary

- Must be standards-based
  - Teacher finds students at:
    - **Below expectations**
    - **At expectations**
    - **Above expectations**
- Results must reveal why some students are scoring below expectations
- Teachers must create student profiles to represent individual assessment
- Teachers must create class profiles to represent class assessment

To differentiate comprehension instruction:

- **For struggling readers:**
  - Help students build their word analysis, fluency, vocabulary, academic knowledge, and background knowledge
  - Either read grade-level text to children or provide audio of text
  - Use concrete examples
- **For English Learners:**
  - Use transfer of L1
  - Explicitly teach comprehension strategies that are missing
- **For advanced learners:**
  - Increase the pace of instruction
  - Use more advanced texts
  - Extend the assignments

QAR

K-1 → In the book
→ In my head
2-6 grade → Right there
→ Think and search
→ Author and You
→ On My Own

SUMMARY

→ Standards based
→ Teacher creates profiles on students
→ Class profiles
→ Explains score

DIFFERENTIATE

STRUGGLING → LEARNERS → ADVANCED

↑ Word Analysis
→ Audio or text
→ Examples.

L1

Instruction
+ Advanced Texts

10. If you need an oral activity to access reading comprehension, which strategy can you use?

Think-Pair-Share or **retelling**

THINK-PAIR-SHARE

RETELLING

11. If you need a written activity to access reading comprehension, which strategy can you use?

Student literature journal or **summary writing**

RicaTest .com

12. How to differentiate reading comprehension of literary instruction?

- **For struggling readers:**
  - Provide audio recordings of text
  - Focus on key story elements
  - Use story maps
  - Reteach necessary skills
- **For English learners:**
  - Clarify cultural differences
  - Pre-teach key vocabulary
- **For advanced learners:**
  - Increase the pace of instruction
  - Use more advanced texts
  - Extend the assignments

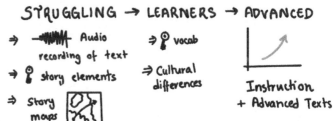

13. What is the difference between skimming and scanning?

- **Skimming**: Fast reading to preview or review a text
- **Scanning:** Rapid reading to find specific information

14. How to teach, assess, and differentiate reading comprehension for expository texts?

Used for teaching AND assessing:

Before reading: Use a graphic organizer

After reading: Use a study guide

Differentiating instruction for:

- **Struggling readers:**
  - Provide audio recordings of text
  - Focus on key content
  - Vocabulary instruction with concrete examples
- **English Learners:**
  - Explicit modeling using think-alouds
  - Using oral language activities to support content-area knowledge
  - Building from L1 background knowledge
- **Advanced learners:**
  - Increase the pace of instruction
  - Use more advanced texts
  - Extend the assignments

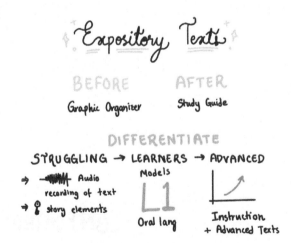

15. What is the Matthew Effect?

Rich get richer; poor get poorer effect, regarding reading: students who learn swift word identification skills and learn to read with automaticity become better students who enjoy reading while students who don't learn these fundamental skills enjoy reading less and therefore read less, which creates a bigger and bigger gap in reading ability, compared to their peers

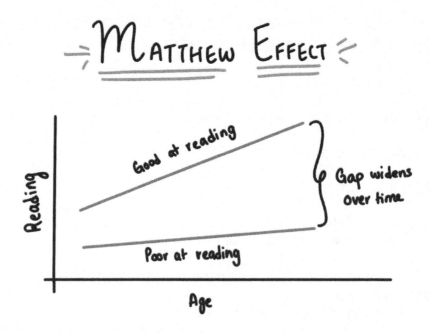

Matthew Effect

Reading (y-axis) / Age (x-axis)

Good at reading

Poor at reading

Gap widens over time

16. What are the four components of vocabulary instruction?

1. Direct instruction of specific words
2. Teaching students independent word-learning strategies
3. Developing word consciousness
4. Encouraging wide reading

COMPONENTS OF VOCABULARY INSTRUCTION

⇒ Direct instruction of specific words
⇒ Independent word-learning strategies
⇒ Word consciousness
⇒ Wide reading

17. What is **word consciousness**?

Developing an interest in words and their meanings

18. The five stages of spelling development are as follows:

1. **Precommunicative**: Students' spelling shows no understanding that letters represent sounds at this stage.

   At this time, students will not write letters, but instead draw pictures or doodles. Moreover, if the child has written letters, they are placed in random order.

2. **Semiphonetic**: Children at this stage use letters to attempt to represent sounds. The child understands that letters represent sounds, but the understanding is poorly developed.

   At this stage, the child may correctly write the first letter of a word, but the rest does not match.

3. **Phonetic**: Children at this stage understand that each letter of a word represents a sound. In the phonetic stage, although students understand that each letter represents a sound, they will often choose the wrong letters to represent the sound they hear when they sound the word out.

RicaTest .com

Teachers at this stage must encourage students to keep writing, as although the student may understand their spelling is not correct, teachers expect the spelling to improve over time.

4. **Transitional**: A child at this stage understands the majority of sound-to-symbol relationships in the English language. They understand that each sound comes from a letter. At the transitional stage, the child is mostly choosing the correct letters to spell words.
5. **Conventional**: At this stage, almost all words written by the student are spelled correctly. At the conventional stage, students are usually able to look at a word and understand if it is spelled incorrectly.

These five stages of spelling development are crucial steps for a student's phonics understanding. Reading fluency is built from swift word identification, which comes from phonics understanding. Furthermore, having a strong grasp for phonics will also help a student's ability to spell words correctly.

For your exam, remember that the test will likely use the phrase **orthographic knowledge** in place for spelling. Moreover, remember that phonics instruction is the skill learned to decode and use orthographic (spelling) patterns found in the English language.

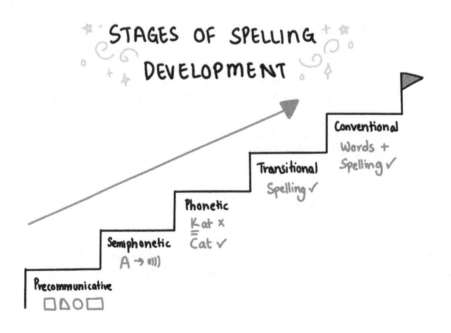

RICA Subtest 2 -
Essay Question Study Guide

Subtest 2 includes a total of two essays, or constructed-response questions, that you'll be asked to compose a 75 to 125-word response for Domain 4's question and a 150- to 300-word response for Domain 5's question, respectively.

Below is a list of student's needs you may find in your RICA test.

*Note- There are multiple instructional strategies that can be used; however, you should choose to write about the one instructional strategy that you feel most comfortable to explain.

Student's needs in and instructional strategies for vocabulary, academic language, and background knowledge:

- **Student's need:** The student is having a difficult time understanding the meaning of words (vocabulary)
  - **Instructional strategy:** Use contextual redefinition
    - Teacher displays text passage that highlights to-be-taught vocabulary
    - Students independently read the passage and write what they think the meaning of the vocabulary words are. If students don't know, they write, I don't know.
    - Students move into small groups of three, share their definitions of the words, and each student is free to change or update their definition
    - Teacher moves instruction back to whole-group, and asks for volunteer students to read their definitions
    - Teacher listens to students and writes definition of the word on the board and the student copies it into their word journal
  - **Benefit**: Teaches target words using the power of cooperative learning

- **Student's need**: Student doesn't have background knowledge about topic
  - **Instructional strategy:** Use KWL chart

- **KWL chart**: Teacher writes KWL on chart paper and separates the three letters with a line, forming three columns. K represents what students know, W for what students want to know, and L for what students want to learn
- **Picture walk**: Teacher has a book and the teacher and students "walk through the book" by looking at the pictures of the story ahead of time to get a gist for what the story is about
- **Set purpose for reading**: Teacher directly and explicitly states, *"Today class, we are going to read about friendship..."*
  - **Benefit**: Provides auditory and visual scaffold and uses power of whole-group cooperation and knowledge

Student needs in and instructional strategies for comprehension:

- **Student's need:** Student is having a difficult time answering comprehension questions during reading
  - **Instructional strategy**: Question Classification/ Answer Verification through use of giving a graphic organizer or study guide
    - **For K-1st grade:**
      - In my head
      - In the book
    - **For 2nd-6th grade:**
      - Right there
      - Think and search
      - Author and me
      - On my own
    - **For middle schoolers**
      - Literal question
      - Inferential question
      - Evaluative question
  - **Benefit:** Eliminates students wasting time trying to figure out what kind of answer they need to provide, i.e. if they can find the answer in the book or not

- **Student's need:** Student is having a hard time comprehending the material after they read
  - **Instructional strategy**: Use a study guide
  - **Benefit:** Provides students with scaffold

RicaTest.com

- **Student's need**: Student is having a hard time with story elements in a narrative text
  - ○ **Instructional strategy**: Use a story grammar outline
    - ■ *Setting:*
    - ■ *Characters:*
    - ■ *Problem:*
      - ● *event 1:*
      - ● *event 2:*
      - ● *event 3:*
    - ■ *Resolution:*
    - ■ *Theme:*
  - ○ **Benefit:** SGO helps students identify literary elements

- **Student's need:** Student is having a difficult time researching a topic in an expository text
  - ○ **Instructional strategy:** Provide student with an outline
  - ○ **Benefit:** Provide student with temporary scaffold to help student gather information

- **Student's need**: Student is having a difficult time summarizing or paraphrasing what they read
  - ○ **Instructional strategy**: Use semantic map (word web)
  - ○ **Benefit:** Helps students organize what they have learned and teaches them a study skill

RICA Subtest 3 Study Guide

To be fully prepared to pass the RICA Subtest 3, which includes RICA Domain 1 (Planning, Organizing, and Managing Reading Instruction Based on Ongoing Assessment), you will want to read this guide carefully to understand the material that will be covered in Subtest 3.

Subtest 3 - Structure

The table below shows that Subtest 3 consists of reading Domain 1, Planning, Organizing, and Managing Reading Instruction Based on Ongoing Assessment.

Domain	Number of competencies	Number of Multiple-Choice Questions	Number and Type of Constructed-Response Questions
Domain 1 (Planning, Organizing, and Managing Reading Instruction Based on Ongoing Assessment)	2	25	1 (Case Study, 300- to 600-word response assessing all domains)
Total	2	25	1

There are a total of two reading competencies to know that will be covered with 25 multiple-choice questions.

Subtest 3 also includes a total of one Case Study question, that you're asked to compose a 300- to 600-word response.

Subtest 3 - Overview

Below, you will find the competencies that make the domain that you must know to pass Subtest 3:

Domain 1: Planning, Organizing, and Managing Reading Instruction Based on Ongoing Assessment

Competency 1: Understand how to plan, organize, and manage standards-based reading instruction.

Competency 2: Understand the purposes of reading assessment and best practices related to standards-based entry-level assessment, monitoring of student progress, and summative assessment.

Subtest 3 - Learning Outcomes

Be able to answer the following questions:

1. What is the goal of standards-based reading instruction?

2. Define what a standard is.

3. State the two aspects, according to *RICA Content Specifications*, that an instructional program in reading and language arts needs to be.

4. Define *differentiated instruction*.

5. *Effective instructional delivery* of content needs to be _____ and _____.

6. List ways to promote and motivate reading in the classroom.

7. Which strategy do we use to promote independent reading?

8. How to promote reading practice in the classroom?

9. How to promote reading practice at home?

10. How to promote at-home reading and support parents of English Learners?

11. How to monitor students' independent reading

12. How to create a support system to promote reading to struggling readers?

13. Define the three types of reading assessments.

14. How to differentiate for students with an Individualized Education Program (IEP) or Section 504 Plan?

15. What does it mean if a standardized test has *reliability?*

16. What does it mean if a standardized test has *validity?*

17. What is the difference between a *percentile score, grade equivalent score,* and *stanine score* in standardized testing?

18. Describe the purpose and use of an *Informal Reading Inventory* (IRI).

19. Define *independent reading level, instructional reading level,* and *frustration reading level.*

20. What is a scaffold and what can a scaffold include?

21. How can a teacher teach students to pick the right level of reading books?

22. How can a teacher organize instruction to meet the needs of all learners?

RICA Subtest 3
Study Guide Answers

1. What is the goal of *standards-based reading instruction*?

Every student will meet the content standards adopted by the California State Board of Education

GOAL OF STANDARDS-BASED READING

Student meets standards set by the California State Board of Education

2. Define what a *standard* is.

A standard states what every student should know and be able to do at each grade level.

A standard is what every student should know and be able to do at each grade level

3. State the two aspects, according to *RICA Content Specifications*, that an instructional program in reading and language arts needs to be.
- *Balanced instruction*: A strategic selection of skills taught throughout the year
- *Comprehensive instruction*: The teacher works to help students achieve all grade-level standards

BALANCED VS. COMPREHENSIVE

Selection of skills

All grade - level standards

4. Define *differentiated instruction*.

Meeting the needs of individual learners, including making adjustments to meet the needs of individual learners.

5. *Effective instructional delivery* of content needs to be
_____ and _____.

Direct and **explicit**

6. List ways to promote and motivate reading in the classroom.
- Providing a stimulating learning environment
    - Using excitement in the classroom
    - Having a classroom library with many books of different types, styles and levels
    - Using bulletin board displays that feature student work
    - Having classroom rules for polite, no-put-down behavior
- Reading aloud to students
- Set up book clubs, literature circles and author studies

7. Which strategy do we use to promote independent reading?

I + I strategy (student's **interest** + student's **independent reading level**)

8. How to promote reading practice in the classroom?

- **Sustained silent reading**
- **Reader's Workshop**

Shh... → Sustained Silent
Reading

→ Reader's Workshop

9. How to promote reading practice at home?
- Allow children to take home books from the classroom library
- Provide a list of books to the parents for their individual child

10. How to promote at-home reading and support parents of English Learners?
- Provide communication to parents in their native language
- Encourage parents to read with their children at home
- Provide a list of books in parent's native language for children to read at home

11.   How to monitor and assess students' independent reading

- Student-maintained reading logs
- Book reports
- Written and oral presentations
- Individual conferences

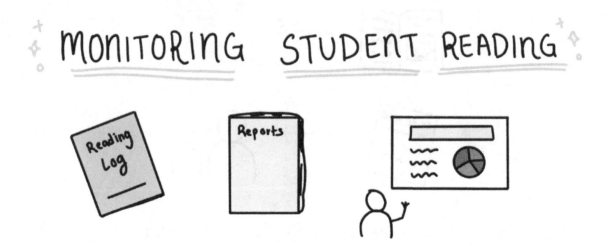

12.   How to create a support system to promote reading for struggling readers?

Facilitate a conference with the student, the student's parents, the reading coach/ learning specialist, and principle to create reading goals

13.   Define the three types of reading assessments

- **Entry-level assessment:** Assessment given prior to instruction to determine which students possess prerequisite skills and knowledge of the topic
- **Monitoring-of-progress assessment:** Assessment given during an instructional unit to better understand which students are and are not making adequate progress toward achieving the target standard
- **Summative assessment:** Assessment given after an instructional unit, quarter, or year to measure student achievement of a specific standard or many standards

ENTRY

⇒ Prior to instruction

⇒ Diagnostic

PROGRESS

⇒ During instructional unit

⇒ Determine Student's performance

SUMMαTIVE

⇒ End of the unit

⇒ Checks achievement of standards

14.   How to differentiate for students with an Individualized Education Program (IEP) or Section 504 Plan?

- Give students more time
- Split up assessment into smaller units
- Provide practice assessment

IEP STUDENTS

More time

Smaller pieces

Practice

RicaTest .com

15.	What does it mean if a standardized test has *reliability?*

A test has reliability if the results yield consistent scores across administrations

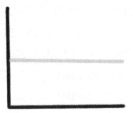

16.	What does it mean if a standardized test has *validity?*

A test has validity if the test measures what it claims to measure

17. What is the difference between a *percentile score*, *grade equivalent score,* and *stanine score* in standardized testing?

- **Percentile score**: A student who has a percentile score of 78 has a higher raw score than 78% of the sampling group. An average score would therefore be a score of 50.
- **Grade equivalent score**: The score gives the performance correspondence to which grade and month the student scored in. For example, if a student scored 78 out of 100, and the grade equivalent score shows 6.4, that means the student scored at the 6th grade, 4th-month level.
- **Stanine score**: The raw score is converted to a 9-point scale.

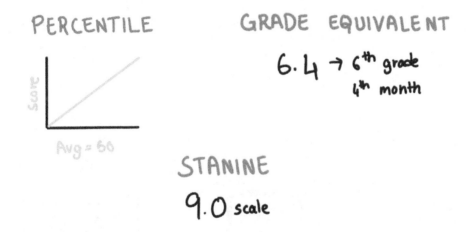

18. Describe the purpose and use of an *Informal Reading Inventory* (IRI)

An IRI is an individualized portfolio of assessments collected over the year to show an individual student's reading level. Assessments often, but do not necessarily include, the following:

- Word recognition lists
- Reading interest surveys
- Concepts about print
- Phonemic awareness
- Fluency
- Structural analysis
- Vocabulary

*Students at different grade levels will have different types of assessments in the IRI

19. Define *independent reading level, instructional reading level,* and *frustration reading level*

- **Independent reading level:** When a student demonstrates the ability to read aloud 95% or more words correctly and answer 90% of comprehension questions correctly
- **Instructional reading level**: When a student demonstrates the ability to read aloud 90-94% of words correctly and answer 60% of comprehension questions correctly
- **Frustration reading level:** When a student demonstrates the ability to read aloud less than 90% of words correctly or answer 60% of the comprehension questions correctly

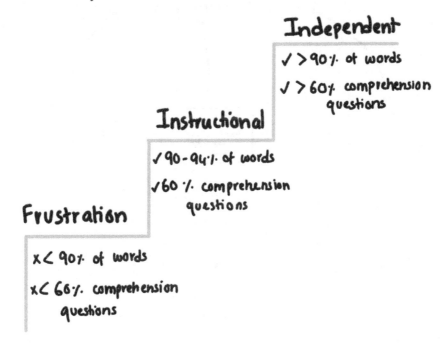

Independent
✓ >90% of words
✓ >60% comprehension questions

Instructional
✓ 90-94% of words
✓ 60% comprehension questions

Frustration
x < 90% of words
x < 60% comprehension questions

20. A **scaffold** is a temporary piece of support that a teacher provides to a student to help them master a task.
   a. A scaffold can be a piece of information that helps guide the student to master of the task
   b. A scaffold can also be a tool, such as a chart, diagram, or illustration to help the student master a task
   c. What's important is that a scaffold is *temporary*.

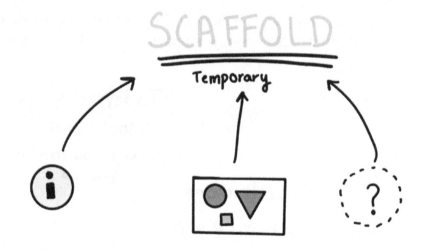

21. There are two simple, yet effective rules that teachers can teach their students to help them choose books at their *just right reading levels.*

    a. The first, is primarily used for students at or under 2nd grade, and that is called the **Goldilocks Test**, which tells students to pick a book which is not too difficult and not too easy.

    b. The second, is primarily used for students at or above 2nd grade, and that is called the **Five-Fingers Test**, where a student will open a book and read a page. For every word the student doesn't know the meaning of or how to pronounce, they put one finger up. If the student reads a page and there is 0 or 1 finger up, the book is too easy. If the student reads a page and they have 4 or 5 fingers up, the book is too difficult. If the student reads a page and 3 fingers up, the book is just right!

It's important to note that if the student feels highly engaged with the content or motivated to read that book, but has found 4 words they don't understand, the student might still be able to appropriately read that book.

Goldilocks
Test

Five Finger
Test

22. How can a teacher organize instruction to meet the needs of all learners?

In order to ensure that all students have met the standard for the skills taught in the classroom, teachers will form **flexible groups and provide individual instruction**

RicaTest.com

Flexible groups are used for students who need to practice a specific skill or strategy, so the teacher can form this group to work more closely with the students who still need to master this skill. Likewise, if there is only one student who has demonstrated that they have not yet mastered a skill taught, the teacher will create individualized instruction to help this student master the skill.

RICA Subtest 3 - Case Study

The case study question material will come from Domain's 2 - 5, so many of the student needs and instructional strategies presented below were also presented above.

Step-by-step instructions to write a passing case study response is presented in full detail in the online course, so be sure to watch, listen and take notes from that resource.

In the case study you will be asked to identify a student's strengths and/or student's needs and then present instructional strategies and the benefits of the instructional strategies to support the student's reading development.

Below is a list of student needs you may find in your RICA test. State which instructional strategy you would use and the benefit of that instructional strategy for the student's reading development.

*There are multiple instructional strategies that can be used, and are listed below, for the same student's need. On the test, when there are multiple instructional strategies that are possible, choose the one you feel most comfortable to explain.

Rica Case Study Map

Memorize this map, and quickly make it on test day to write a fully accurate response.

Domain	Task 1: Str./need	Task 2: Instr. Strat.	Task 3: Benefit
Domain 2: word analysis			
Pa		Sound Seg.	helps teach word sounds
CAP		Shared book exp.	Teaches meaning, reppres D.v. Book hand.
Let Rec		tactik/kin	learn letters swiftly/acc.
Ph/sw		whole-to-part	7 gram. Sound-symb. relat.
SY/ST Ana		whole-to-part	SS decode root + affix
SP		multi sensory instruct	rep./aud/vis.
Domain 3: Fluency			
flu		monitored oral Reading	╳
• acc.		Repeated reading	builds word i.d.
• rate.		whisper reading	builds word i.d.
• Pros.		Phrase-cued Reading	build word i.v.
Domain 4: VALBK			
voc. (in conx)		contextual redef.	Teach vocab using conX + coop learng
al (lu isolatio)		word map	learn meaning activ. Bk know
bk		KWL chart	make connex -ss -text -world
Domain 5: Comp.			
Comp. nar —		Story grammar outline	Provide(s) vis. Lit. ele.
comp. info { Bef. Dur. Aft.		graphic org study guide	Directs SS to key info

Student's needs in and instructional strategies for phonemic awareness:

- **Student's need:** The student is having a difficult time identifying how many words are in a sentence
  - **Instructional strategy**: Build word awareness skills
    - Teacher uses several cards, each having one word written on it
    - Teacher creates two-word sentences, *Jack walks*
    - Teacher and student read sentence together
    - Teacher splits sentence up by words
    - Teacher asks student, "How many words are in the sentence?"
    - Teacher builds off sentence and adds a word to create three-word sentence, *Jack walks fast*
    - Teacher asks, "How many words are in the sentence?"
  - **Benefit:** Helps children become aware that sentences are made up of words

- **Student's need:** The student is having a difficult time identifying syllables in a word
  - **Instructional strategy**: Build syllable awareness skills
    - Teach children to clap their hands as they say each syllable in a word
    - Pronounce words slowly and elongate word pronunciation
  - **Benefit:** Helps children become aware that words are made up of syllables

- **Student's need**: The student is having difficulty with compound words
  - **Instructional strategy**: Build word blending skills
    - Teacher has pictures of the two parts of the compound word (foot, ball)
    - Teacher prompts, "This is a picture of a foot, and this is a picture of a ball, what do you get when you put them together?" (football)
  - **Benefit:** Helps children visually see compound words

- **Student's need:** The student is having difficulty reading multisyllabic words
  - ○ **Instructional strategy:** Build syllable blending skills
    - ■ Teacher says, "What word do we give if we put *bro* and *ther* together?" (brother)
  - ○ **Benefit:** Helps students put multisyllabic words together

- **Student's need:** The student is having difficulty identifying the sounds at the beginning, middle, or end of a word
  - ○ **Instructional strategy:** Build sound isolation skills
    - ■ Teacher picks a list of words with common elements that student has shown a need to improve, such as words with the long a sound
    - ■ Teacher models the correct pronunciation of the word and says the sound of the problem element, in the case the long a sound
    - ■ Teacher says a word (more challenging if the student needs to read the word), and the student pronounces the word, and gives the beginning, middle, or ending sound (whichever the lesson is focused on)
  - ○ **Benefit:** Helps students break up sounds of a word

- **Student's need:** The student is having a difficult time reading multisyllabic words
  - ○ **Instructional strategy:** Build sound blending skills
    - ■ Teacher says sounds of words with brief pauses between each sound, /c/, /a/, /t/
    - ■ Teacher says, "Which word am I thinking of?" (cat)
  - ○ **Benefit:** Helps students properly pronounce new words

- **Student's need:** The student is having a difficult time isolating and identifying the sounds in a spoken word
  - ○ **Instructional strategy:** Build sound segmentation skills
    - ■ Teacher starts by gathering a list of words with only two sounds
    - ■ Teacher models desired behavior by saying, "I am going to say a word and then say the sounds in the word."
      - ● *Bee, /b/, /e/*
    - ■ Once student demonstrates ability with two-sound words, teacher uses words with three sounds
      - ● *Cat, /c/, /a/, /t/*

RicaTest .com

o **Benefit:** Helps students segment new words

Student's needs in and instructional strategies for concepts about print:

- **Student's need:** The student is having a difficult time with awareness between the relationship that print carries meaning, letter, word, and sound representation, directionality of print, AND/OR book-handling skills
  - **Instructional strategy:** Use shared book experience
    - Teacher uses a Big Book and starts by introducing the cover, author's name, title, title page, and other aspects of the book
    - Teacher reads story with full dramatic punch. Teacher pauses for predictions
    - Teacher and students have a discussion about the book, sharing their favorite parts
    - Story is reread at a later time, where students can reenact parts of the story
  - **Benefit:** Helps students improve all aspects of concepts about print

- **Student's need:** The student is having a difficult time recognizing, naming and/or writing specific letters
  - **Instructional strategy:** Use tactile and kinesthetic methods, such as when kids use modeling clay to make letters. This method also works great for struggling readers
  - **Benefit:** Hands-on approach to better understanding and becoming familiar with letters

- **Student's need:** The student is mixing up similar letters, such as p, d, q, and/or b
  - **Instructional strategy:** Use tactile, kinesthetic, auditory and visual methods

- Teacher models and provides students practice to trace and write the target letters while students say out loud the direction it takes to make the letter. This can be done on screens to make the activity tactile, can be done in the air to make the activity kinesthetic, and can be done using different colored crayons or colored pencils to make the activity visual
  - **Benefit:** Hands-on approach to better understanding and becoming familiar with letters

- **Student's need:** The student is having a difficult time with phonics and/or sight words
  - **Instructional strategy**: Use whole-to-part phonics/ sight word instruction (see above for specific directions)
  - **Benefit:** Gives students systematic, direct and explicit instruction toward understanding the relationship between sound-to-writing of language

- **Student's need:** The student is struggling with root words or affixes (prefixes/ suffixes)
  - **Instructional strategy**: Use whole-to-part structural analysis instruction (see above for specific directions)
  - **Benefit:** Gives students systematic, direct and explicit instruction toward understanding the parts of a written word

- **Student's need**: The student is struggling with spelling
  - **Instructional strategy:** Use Multisensory Instruction
    - Students having a difficult time spelling should write the target word(s) multiple times using different colors by highlighting the target vowels (boat) [visual] while saying each word out loud [auditory]
  - **Benefit:** Caters to student's senses to help remember spelling better

- **Student's need**: The student isn't motivated about reading
  - **Instructional strategy**: Use I + I strategy (student's **interest** + student's **independent reading level**)

RicaTest .com

- ○ **Benefit:** Caters to student's interest

Student's needs in and instructional strategies for fluency:

- **Student's need:** The student needs to improve reading fluency
  - ○ **Instructional strategy**: Use Monitored Oral Reading
  - ○ **Benefit:** Provides student with modeling, practice and feedback

- **Student's need:** The student needs to improve reading fluency, specifically with accuracy
  - ○ **Instructional strategy:** Use Monitored Oral Reading
    - ■ **Build word identification skills**, such as phonics and sight words
  - ○ **Benefit:** Provides student with modeling, practice and feedback

- **Student's need:** The student needs to improve reading fluency, specifically with rate
  - ○ **Instructional strategy:** Use Monitored Oral Reading
    - ■ Whisper reading
  - ○ **Benefit:** Encourages reading, even for shy/embarrassed readers

- **Student's need:** The student needs to improve reading fluency, specifically with prosody
  - ○ **Instructional strategy:** Use Monitored Oral Reading
    - ■ Phrase-cued reading
      - • Teacher makes marks in text passage
        - ○ / = comma; // = period
      - • Students with the same independent reading level come together in small group
      - • Students practice reading using teacher's markings for proper prosody
  - ○ **Benefit:** Provides student with modeling, practice and feedback

Student's needs in and instructional strategies for **vocabulary, academic language, and background knowledge:**

- **Student's need:** The student having a difficult time understanding the meaning of words (vocabulary)
  - ○ **Instructional strategy:** Use contextual redefinition
    - ■ Teacher displays text passage that highlights to-be-taught vocabulary
    - ■ Students independently read the passage and write what they think the meaning of the vocabulary words are. If students don't know, they write, I don't know.
    - ■ Students move into small groups of three, share their definitions of the words, and each student is free to change or update their definition
    - ■ Teacher moves instruction back to whole-group, and asks for volunteer students to read their definitions
    - ■ Teacher listens to students and writes definition of the word on the board and the student copies it into their word journal
  - ○ **Benefit:** Teaches target words using the power of cooperative learning

- **Student's need:** Student doesn't have background knowledge about topic
  - ○ **Instructional strategy:** Use KWL chart
    - ■ **KWL chart:** Teacher writes KWL on chart paper and separates the three letters with a line, forming three columns. K represents what students know, W for what students want to know, and L for what students want to learn
    - ■ **Picture walk:** Teacher has a book and the teacher and students "walk through the book" by looking at the pictures of the story ahead of time to get a gist for what the story is about
    - ■ **Set purpose for reading:** Teacher directly and explicitly states, *"Today class, we are going to read about friendship..."*
  - ○ **Benefit:** Provides auditory and visual scaffold and uses power of whole-group cooperation and knowledge

- **Student's need:** Student is having a difficult time answering comprehension questions during reading
    - **Instructional strategy**: Question Classification/ Answer Verification through use of giving a graphic organizer or study guide
        - **For K-1st grade:**
            - In my head
            - In the book
        - **For 2nd-6th grade:**
            - Right there
            - Think and search
            - Author and me
            - On my own
        - **For middle schoolers**
            - Literal question
            - Inferential question
            - Evaluative question
    - **Benefit:** Eliminates students wasting time trying to figure out what kind of answer they need to provide, i.e. if they can find the answer in the book or not

- **Student's need:** Student is having a hard time comprehending the material after they read
    - **Instructional strategy**: Use a study guide
    - **Benefit:** Provides students with scaffold

- **Student's need**: Student is having a hard time with story elements in a narrative text
    - **Instructional strategy**: Use a story grammar outline
        - *Setting:*
        - *Characters:*
        - *Problem:*
            - *event 1:*
            - *event 2:*
            - *event 3:*
        - *Resolution:*
        - *Theme:*
    - **Benefit:** SGO helps students identify literary elements

 RicaTest .com

- **Student's need:** Student is having a difficult time researching a topic in an expository text
  - ○ **Instructional strategy:** Provide student with an outline
  - ○ **Benefit:** Provides student with temporary scaffold to help students gather information

- **Student's need:** Student is having a difficult time summarizing or paraphrasing what they read
  - ○ **Instructional strategy:** Use semantic map (word web)
  - ○ **Benefit:** Helps students organize what they have learned and teaches them a study skill

Rica Test Vocabulary Terms

ABC books: An important tool in teaching the alphabet to young learners. ABC books are books presenting all the letters of the English alphabet.

Academic language: A key component for teaching vocabulary instruction, this is also called the language of the classroom.

Accuracy: The ability to pronounce words correctly.

Advanced learners: Students who score above one grade level on a standardized test to the actual grade that they're in.

Affix: A morpheme that, when alone, is not a word, and appears only as a part of a word. There are two types: prefixes and suffixes.

Alphabetic principle: The speech sounds that are represented by letters.

Analytic phonics: Also called, Whole-to-part phonics instruction. In this approach, instruction begins with the identification of a familiar word or sentence. The teacher then introduces a particular sound/spelling relationship within that familiar word.

Antonym contextual clue: When a student seeks to understand the meaning of a word by scouting around that word and finding an antonym (a word with the opposite meaning)

Antonyms: Two words with opposite meanings (big and small).

Auditorily similar letters: Two letters that sound alike (p and d)

Author studies: Readers who read books by one author and the students discuss the author's style of writing

Automaticity: This is the goal of all reading instruction, and it occurs when the reader does not stop to decode words, instead, they read smoothly and fluently.

Automaticity theory: A reading theory that requires readers to be able to
   1) decode words, and
   2) understand the meaning of the text

Background knowledge: All that a person knows about a topic

Balanced instructional program in reading: A reading program that provides a mixture of direct reading instruction and strategies with opportunities for students to practice. This kind of instructional reading program is one that has these three things: 1) instructional materials (texts and assessments), 2) reading skills and strategies students are expected to master, 3) instructional strategies to teach these skills and strategies

Basal reading programs: A commercially produced package of instructional materials used to teach children to read, using graduated sets of reading texts

Blends: Two- or three-letter combinations of consonants that are pronounced together to make a sound. (bl in blend)

Book club: A group of students reading the same book at the same pace

Bound morpheme: An affix that only exists when attached to a word (pre in pretest)

Cause and effect: A text structure used in expository texts to show how one phenomenon results from another phenomenon

Character: The who of the story- in children's books, characters can be people, but also animals, plants, and inanimate objects

Closed syllable: A syllable that ends with a consonant

Cognates: Two words from different languages that have similar spellings and meanings

Compare and contrast: An expository text structure frequently used to describe the differences, and even similarities (using a Venn diagram) of a place, person, or thing

Complex sentence: A type of sentence that has one independent clause and one dependent clause, and are linked with the words, because, since, after, although, when, that, who, or which (Fred kicked the football to Sam, who kicked it over the fence.)

Compound sentence: A type of sentence that has two independent clauses and are joined by words that include, and, nor, but, yet, and so (Fred kicked the football and Sally played on the swings.)

Comprehension: Having an understanding of what was just read

Comprehensive reading program: A reading program structured so that all grade-level standards are covered

Concepts about print (CAP): A key component to a kindergartener's reading instruction, These are the essential principles and formats of letters, words, and sentences in a written language. There are four main areas of CAP. These include, 1) understanding that print carries meaning and that there is a relationship between spoken and written English 2) the ability to recognize the differences between letters 3) the directionality of print (left to right and top to bottom) 4) book handling skills

Concepts about print test: A test that measures a child's mastery of concepts about print

Concrete examples: Using real things in a lesson to show, demonstrate and teach the meaning of the word (banana)

Consonants: Speech sounds that occur when the airflow is obstructed in some way by our mouth, teeth, or lips

Content-area literacy: The reading and writing of expository texts

Context clues: Words or phrases around the target word that can help the reader understand the target word

Contextual analysis: Used with upper-elementary students to find the meaning of a word. This is when a student looks at the context, which can include
  1) definition
  2) synonym
  3) antonym
  4) example

Conventional stage of spelling development: The fifth and final stage of spelling development. Mistakes only happen with irregular words, such as soverenty for sovereignty

Coordinators: Words used to join independent clauses (for, and, nor, but, yet, so)

Data retrieval chart: Prepared by teacher and used by students when reading and gathering data from an expository text

Decodable text: Texts written for young learners using single-syllable words (Dan has a red fan.)

Definition contextual clue: A clue provided by the author to the reader to understand a new word. These are often used in expository texts, like social studies and science textbooks

Dependent clause: A phrase with a subject and verb, but cannot stand on its own and therefore, is not a sentence

Differentiated instruction: A way of teaching that recognizes individual student differences, where the teacher makes adjustments to the lesson or designs unique lessons based on the needs of the learner

Digraphs: Two-letter combinations that have one sound (ph in phone)

Diphthongs: Glided sounds made by vowel combinations, such as oi in oil or ou in about

Direct, explicit instruction: Teacher-directed lessons with a clearly defined learning objective

Entry-level assessments: As assessment given prior to teaching the unit to see students' current mastery of the standard, skill, or strategy

96

Environmental print: Printed material found in daily living, such as on a bumper sticker, candy wrapper, or restaurant menu

Etymology: Study of origin of words

Evaluative comprehension: The ability of a reader to make judgments about what has been read (answers to these comprehension questions are not in book, but rather require students to think about and make a judgment)

Example contextual clue: A clue a reader uses to figure out the meaning of a target word. The learner understands the meaning of the target word through the example that the author provides- example Mammals are many types of animals, that include dogs, cows, and bears.

Expository texts: A text that provides information, rather than a story

Figurative language: Giving words meaning beyond their everyday means. This includes, hyperbole, metaphor, personification, and simile

Fluency: The ability to read with appropriate rate, accuracy and prosody

Foreshadowing: The author drops a hint about what might happen in the future

Free morpheme: A morpheme that is a word by itself (test)

Frustration reading level: The grade level of texts that a child cannot read or understand even with the assistance of a teacher. When the student's oral reading fails to achieve 90% accuracy or cannot answer 60% of the comprehension questions correctly, this marks as the student's frustration reading level

Genre: A category of literature

Graded reading passages: A set of texts usually around 50 to 100 words in length, where the student reads them either orally or silently, depending on the objective of the assessment, and helps a teacher determine the student's frustration, instructional, and independent reading levels and also helps identify a student's reading strengths and needs

Grade equivalent scores: A norm-referenced test score that helps translate a student's test score into the grade-level placement, for example 6.3 would translate into 6th grade 3rd month

Gradual release of responsibility: Helps teach reading strategies where teacher first models strategies and eventually students can do the strategies/task themselves (I do, we do, you do)

Graphic features: charts, maps, diagrams, illustrations

Grapheme: Smallest written unit of language

Graphic organizer: Diagram or chart created by teacher, given to students before they read an expository text, and summarizes main points of texts

Graphophonemic error: Symbol-sound error students can make when reading aloud. Example, a student reads feather, but word is father

Guided practice: When students work under close supervision of teacher

High fantasy: A genre of literature that often sets in a fantasy world and portrays the plot of good vs. evil (Harry Potter)

High-frequency words: Words that most often appear in texts

Homographs: Two words with the same spelling but have different pronunciation (wind, wind)

Hyperbole: An exaggerated comparison (He was as big as a house)

Idiom: A phrase that has a meaning that is different from the literal meaning (raining cats and dogs)

I + I strategy: An instructional strategy to enhance a child's level of independent reading using the student's independent reading level and personal interests to find books that are just right for them

Independent reading level: The reading level a child can read and understand without the assistance of the teacher. Marked by a student's ability to accurately read aloud 90% or more of the text and answer 60% or more of the comprehension questions

In-depth reading: When the reader slows down to read more carefully to better understand that section of the text

Individualized Educational Program (IEP): A document required by the federal Individuals with Disabilities Education Act (IDEA) which gives each child with disabilities interventions to help the student succeed in school

Inferential comprehension: The ability of the reader to interpret a text. (Answers to these comprehension questions are not in the text, but rather come from the head of the reader)

Informal reading inventory: The collection of reading assessments given to students and should list the student's frustration and independent reading level, their reading interest and their reading strength and need

Instructional conversations: Used mainly for English Learners, this is when a group of students reads the same text and talks about it

Instructional reading level: The grade-level text that a child can read and understand with the assistance of the teacher

Interest inventory: A survey given to a student to learn about the student's reading interests and behavior

Irony: A stylistic-written device used when there is a difference between what a character says or does and the reality of the situation

KWL chart: An instructional tool that helps children activate their prior knowledge of a topic. This stands for what do you Know, what do you Want to know, and what did you Learn

Language experience approach: An instructional activity where the child dictates to the teacher a personal experience (a trip to the zoo), while the teacher writes verbatim what the student says

L-controlled vowels: Vowel sounds that are neither long nor short (a in chalk/ e in help) and the vowel precedes a consonant

Letter formation: The ability to write the letters of the alphabet so that a reader can easily read them

Letter naming: The ability to correctly say the name of a letter when the teacher points to that letter

Letter recognition: The ability for a student to correctly point to the letter that the teacher has said

Literal comprehension: The ability of a reader to understand the surface meaning of a text

Literary elements: The components of a story: character, plot, setting, mood, theme, and style

Literature circle: A group of students reading the same book that the student's chose

Literature journals: A journal maintained by a student that includes writings about the texts they have read

Matthew effect: The widening of the read ability gap due to the child doesn't like to read, so they don't read, and therefore don't grow developmentally into good readers (rich get richer, poor get poorer)

Meaning vocabulary: All of the words a person understands when they read

Metaphor: Figurative language that is a comparison and does not use a linking word such as like, as, or than (The road was a river of moonlight.)

Miscue Analysis: A process of analyzing a student's oral reading to help identify a student's areas of strength and need so that the teacher can then provide data-based instruction knowing where that student especially needs to work on. (Fred has trouble with words using the CVCe pattern, like bike.)

Monitoring of progress assessment: Assessment that takes place during the sequence of lessons to determine which students are making adequate progress toward achieving the reading standard, skill, or strategy

Morpheme: A unit of meaning- elephant has 1 morpheme (elephant). Unkindly has 3 morphemes (un + kind + ly)

Multisensory techniques: Approaches to teaching writing, spelling and phonics that uses visual, auditory, kinesthetic, tactile or imagery tools

Narrative text: Any text that tells a story, including biography or autobiography

Nontechnical academic language: words and phrases that appear in several disciplines (theory, hypothesis, analysis and synthesis)

Onsets and rimes: These always occur in a single syllable. This is the first consonant of a word and the following part of a word

Open syllable: A SYLLABLE (not just a word) that ends with a vowel. Example: Be and in redesign (re is an open syllable)

Orthographic knowledge: What a person knows about how to spell words- (spelling)

Part-to-whole phonics: The teacher first presents a letter(s) as the target sound. Then, the teacher displays words with the target sound. Finally, the teacher shows these words in a sentence. (part-to-whole phonics is also called synthetic phonics)

Personification: Figurative language which the author gives human traits to nonhuman living things or inanimate objects (The moon laughed at Harry)

Phoneme: A speech sound in a language that signals a difference in meaning. These are the smallest units of speech. Example: /v/ in vote

Phonemic awareness: The ability to distinguish the separate phonemes (sounds) in a spoken word. Example: dog has 3 sounds /d/, /o/, /g/

Phonetically irregular word: Words that do not follow normal sound-symbol relationships. Sometimes they are high frequency words such as, of and the, other times they are words like, great and love; however, all of these words should be taught as sight words.

List the stages of spelling development: precommunicative, semiphonetic, phonetic, transitional, and conventional

Phonics: A part of reading instruction that helps children make the correct association between the sounds and written letters of a language. These types of lessons help children decode words.

Phonological awareness: Knowledge that oral English is composed of smaller units. This is the greater umbrella that holds phonemic awareness, word awareness, and syllabic awareness

Picture walk: A pre-reading activity used with young readers, where the teacher and the students walk through the book before reading it to look and discuss about the pictures that they see to activate the reader's background knowledge of a topic

Pitch: In speaking or oral reading, this is the highness or lowness of the pronunciation of a sound

Plot: The sequence of events in a story

Pre-communication stage of spelling development: The first stage of spelling development. The child's written texts show no understanding that letters represent sounds. The child writes pictures and squiggles

Prefix: An affix that appears in front of a root word

PreP: This is an instructional strategy that helps children activate their background knowledge about a topic.

Preprimer and primer: Two kindergarten reading levels that feature the easiest texts to read

Prosody: One of the three elements of fluency. Prosody is the ability to read with appropriate expression

Question-Answer relationship: A four-level taxonomy used to categorize comprehension questions. The levels are
    1) right there
    2) think and search
    3) author and you
    4) on my own

Question classification/ answer verification: A comprehension-building strategy to increase students' ability to answer correctly all types of comprehension questions- mostly those that are inferential or evaluative

Rate: One element of fluency. This is the speed at which a student reads. Ideally the student should read not too fast and not too slow

R-controlled vowels: Vowel sounds that are neither long nor short, as in car and the word has an r in it

Reciprocal teaching: A comprehension-building strategy used for teaching predicting, generating questions, clarifying and summarizing- This type of teaching follows the gradual release of responsibility model

Reliability: The degree to which an assessment produces consistent scores across administrations

Scaffold: Assistance provided by the teacher that helps a child complete a task

Scanning: Rapid reading to find specific information

Section 504 plan: When a child has a disability but does not qualify for an IEP that describes the necessary interventions a child will receive and who will provide them

Semantic error: When a student reads a synonym of the target word instead of the actual target word. The student reads father but dad is actually written

Semantic maps: Also known as a Word Map- a diagram that shows the relationship among words

Semiphonetic stage of spelling development: Second spelling development, where children at this stage of spelling understanding use letters to represent sounds. The understanding of the sound to symbol relationship is at the beginning stage and a student my spell banana like baa

Sequence: An expository text structure often used in social studies and science textbooks to represent a list of items in numerical or chronological order. Common example is the life cycle of a butterfly

Setting: A literary element that includes both time and place of the story

Shared book experience: An instructional activity for young children where the teacher uses a big book with large print and big pictures to enhance a love of books, teach concepts about print and/or word identification

Sight vocabulary: All the words a child can pronounce correctly

Sight words: Words taught to students as a complete unit and to be memorized by sight

Simile: Figurative language that compares two things linked by words, like, as, or than (He was as big as a house.)

Simple sentence: A sentence that has one subject and one verb (Fred ate all the spaghetti.)

Skimming: A fast reading of a text, usually for the purposes of review or preview

Sound blending: A phonemic awareness task where children blend sounds into a single-syllable word. Example, /b/ /a/ /t/ is bat

Sound deletion: When a student identifies a new word if one sound in a word is deleted. Example: /b/ block, take the b out, what word can you create? lock, shock, mock, tock, etc..

Sound identity: A phonemic awareness task where the child identifies a sound shared by a set of single-syllable words with no other shared sounds. Example: what sound is shared by bike, bake, and bend? /b/

Sound isolation: A phonemic awareness task where a child is given a word and identifies which sound occurs at the beginning, middle, or end of the word. Example: what is the first sound you hear in cake? /k/

Sound segmentation: A phonemic awareness where a child identifies, in order, each sound in a word with two or three sounds. Example: Cap- what are the sounds in cap? /k/ /a/ /p/

Sound substitution: A phonemic awareness task where a child substitutes a sound in a word to make a new word. Example: "Cat, cat, cat- what new word do we get if we take out the /k/ and put in /b/? Bat

Standardized test: A test where the testing format does not vary, except for children with disabilities

Story grammar outline: An outline of a story based to help develop literal comprehension

Story map: A visual representation of a plot in a story used to develop literal comprehension

Structural analysis: Identifying and recognizing words by looking at their prefixes, suffixes, and root words

Struggling reader: A student who's reading score is more than one grade-level below their actual grade

Suffix: An affix that appears at the end of a root word (ly in likely)

Summative assessments: Assessments given at the end of an instructional unit to determine if whether or not a student has mastered a reading standard, skill, or strategy

Sustained silent reading (SSR): A time during the day when the students and the teacher all read silently

Syllabic analysis: The process of identifying and recognizing words by analyzing syllables.

Syllable: A word or part of a word that is pronounced in a single sound

Synonym contextual clue: A clue a reader can use to figure out the meaning of a target word

Syntactic error: Oral reading error when the student substitutes a word that is the same part of speech as the target word. Example: when a student reads into but the text says through. Student understands the meaning but did not apply their knowledge of phonics

Syntax: The order of words in a sentence

Tactile and kinesthetic methods: A teaching method that utilizes instruction with touch and physical motion to provide students with new ways of learning

Technical academic language: Word and phrases related to a specific discipline (constitutional monarchy)

Transitional stage of spelling development: 4th stage in spelling development, where the child knows most of the sound-symbol relationships and understands common spelling patterns.

Validity: The degree to which an assessment accurately measures what it claims to measure

Whole-to-part phonics: An approach to teaching phonics in which the teacher first presents a sentence, then focuses student attention on a target word in the sentence, then highlights a target sound-symbol relationship in the target word

Word analysis: The process of examining the elements and structure of a word

Word identification: The ability to accurately read aloud words- does not mean student understands meaning

Word recognition: Ability to decode a word, meaning student understands meaning of the word

Polysyllabic words: Words with two or more syllables

Describe the difference between inflection, derivations, and roots:
1. Inflection is changing a word by adding an affix.
2. Derivation is forming a new word by adding an affix
    a. example: kick (root) + er (derivation) + s (inflection)

Describe the difference between homophone, homograph, and homonym
   Homophone = two words with the same sound (sight/site)
1. Homograph = two words with the same spelling (wind, wind)
2. Homonym = two words that sound alike but have different spellings and different meanings

What instructional strategy should be used if a student is having a hard time telling letters p, b; d, q apart? Use multisensory techniques. Child is having a difficult

time because the student's visual isn't currently sufficient. Have students write in sand, write in air

Describe the difference between a digraph and a blend: A digraph, which the ph in digraph is a digraph means two letters that make one sound ph = /f/

A blend is two letters that are sounded out together, but you can hear both letters. The word blend has two blends in it= bl and nd.

Have questions?

If you have a question, find a mistake in this guide, or want to reach out to share that you passed your Rica Test, we'd love to hear from you! Send your email to support@ricatest.com.

BEST OF LUCK
ON PASSING YOUR RICA TEST!!

☐ ☐ ☐ You've got this!

Made in the USA
Las Vegas, NV
16 May 2024

90008431R00059